The Market

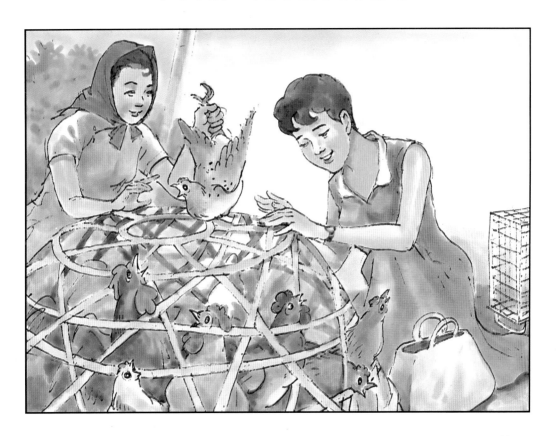

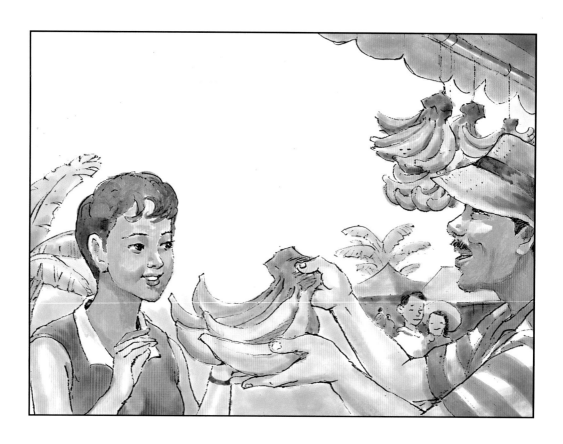

Mom went to the market
to buy five bananas.

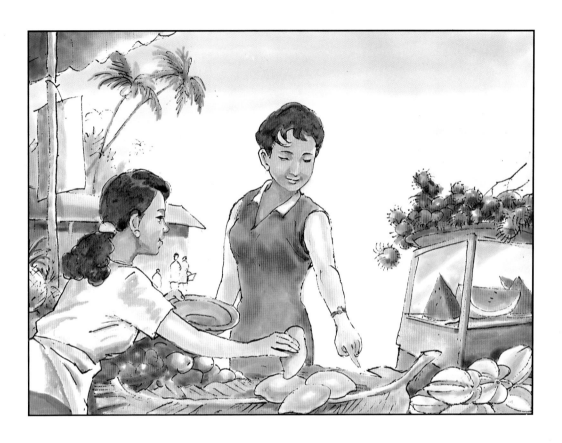

Mom went to the market
to buy four mangoes.

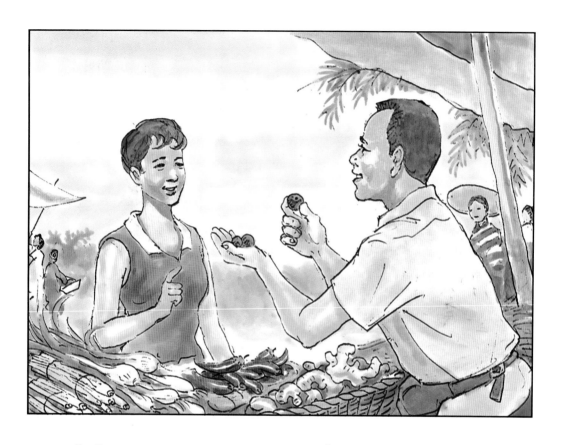

Mom went to the market
to buy three limes.

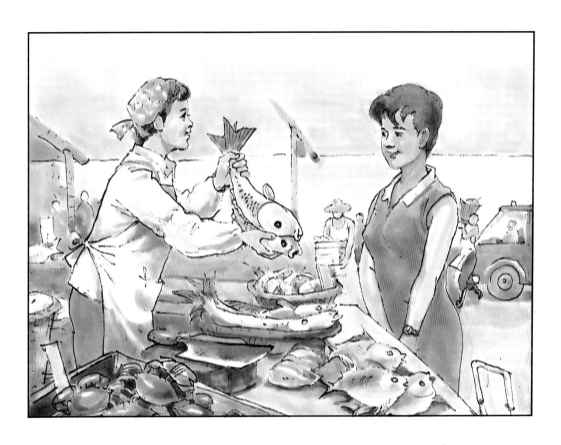

Mom went to the market
to buy two fish.

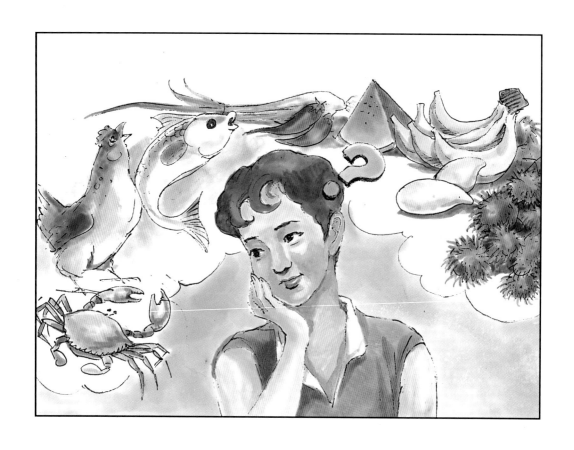

Mom went to the market.

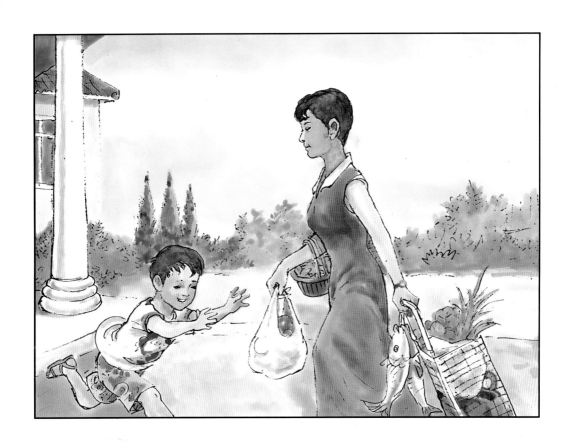

What did Mom buy?

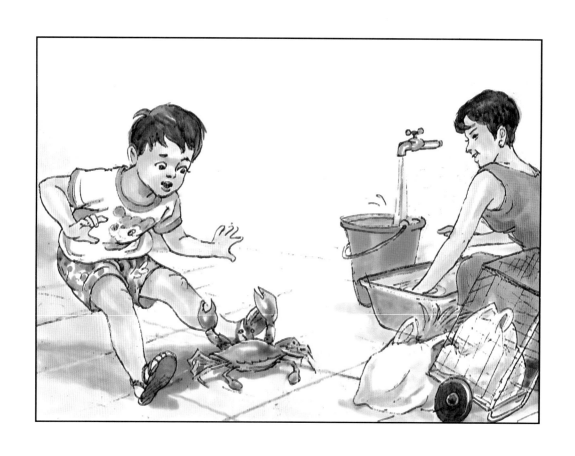

One big crab!